My colourful kitchen

Dwynwen Hopcroft

Copyright © 2012 Dwynwen Hopcroft

All rights reserved.

ISBN -10: 1717092853
ISBN-13:978-1717092854

"When we try to pick out anything by itself, we find it hitched to everything else in the Universe."

John Muir, My First Summer in the Sierra (1911)

CONTENTS

	Acknowledgments	i
1	How to use this book	2
2	Equipment List	6
3	Mordants	8
4	Preparing your Yarn	10
5	Red	12
6	Orange	16
7	Yellow	20
8	Green	24
9	Blue	28
10	Indigo and Violet	32

ACKNOWLEDGMENTS

All my love and sincere thanks to Toby, Margaret, Rhiannon.
Charlotte, Hazel, Dianne, Rosie.
Dani and all the staff at Cafe82.

1 HOW TO USE THIS BOOK

I've been knitting, sewing and generally making a colourful mess for as long as I can remember. I'm very fortunate to have a patient mother that taught me a few skills and tolerated my clothing experiments.

I was 10 when I first became interested in the environment, heartbreaking images of the *Exxon Valdez* oil spill in Alaska were on the BBC Newsround programme and made a huge impact on me. Up until that point I thought that humans had a fairly balanced and benevolent relationship with animals and the Natural world. This was based on living rurally and knowing many farming families. I simply could not understand these images of the massive scale of destruction by humans. Later that year I remember being laughed out of a classroom when trying to present my topic 'Taking Care of the Planet' and from then on being the subject of many classroom jokes for my interests in recycling, which was not mainstream at the time. To be fair I was probably preaching, in that way that teenagers tend to do, but I'm so pleased to see just how much our ideas about reducing waste and working sustainably have become more widely accepted.

So it's been very natural to me when setting up my business Loch Ness Knitting to explore ways of reducing waste and working sustainably. This way of thinking also comes naturally to life in the Scottish Highlands. Large shops are further away so journeys are planned wisely, many items cannot be found locally and are only available online but then incur high delivery charges. Trying to make the very best use of everything you have isn't just great for the planet, it's great for your pocket!

I took a course in natural dyeing to educate and improve my techniques and I found out about many exotic ingredients, but as tempting as these were I just couldn't justify importing them to my business. Instead I found out more about kitchen and garden dyeing and carried out many many dyeing experiments. I looked around for local sources and thanks to my YouTube channel Loch Ness Living I was coming into contact with likeminded businesses who were interested in trying something new. So I have formed a relationship with local cafes and offices to ensure that I have a regular and sustainable source of materials such as avocado and coffee grounds. This reduces waste and makes the very best use of items that are not grown locally, but have travelled a long way to be used around Loch Ness.

One way to adapt this for your own dyeing would be look at the produce section of your local supermarket to pick up fruit and veg for free or at reduced prices. Battered squishy produce might not be good for selling, but is definitely ok for dyeing, as long as it's not visibly brown or mouldy.

Natural dyeing is a great fit with the philosophy that one persons rubbish is another person's treasure, an annoying stain or waste item for the cook can be an intriguing opportunity for the dyer.

This book is designed to inspire natural dye experiments from your own kitchen using familiar kitchen ingredients. By natural dyeing I mean making the dye yourself directly from a plant source. Personally I prefer not to use animal or insects, such as cochineal, as a source of natural dye. Adding dyeing to your kitchen skills reduces waste and introduces a second or third use to the life cycle of ingredients.

The book is organized into colours of the rainbow as most people start dyeing yarn with a particular colour in mind. Please be aware that natural dyeing does not produce the same results as artificial dyes, think more pastels than brights. However for more intense colours you can experiment with different mordants and keep overdyeing to layer up colour.

Natural dyeing also has a reputation for varied and unpredictable results. This can be due to the water, the pans used and variation in the ingredients. Common mistakes are being too hard on the dye bath by overheating, over or under using a mordant, not preparing a high concentration of dye, taking the yarn out too quickly. I've tried to include the easiest and most reliable dye options here to help you get started. If you are still feeling hesitant try dyeing smaller yarn amounts, such as 10-20g mini skeins as testers. I've also included an example of common techniques such as modifying or colour changing the dye. I encourage you to keep your own notes so that you have a record of what worked well for you in your kitchen. Experiment by trying different mordants, overdyeing, and repeated dyeing until the dye bath is exhausted to give a gradually fading range of yarn colours.

We start each colour with a great recipes to help you gather materials and make the connection to the lifecycle of the dye ingredients. All the recipes are vegetarian and gluten free because that's how I roll. After the cooking and when the dye bath is exhausted you can add the waste material to your compost heap and continue the beautiful cycle of sustainable natural dyeing. Although the dye bath is natural please DO NOT attempt to eat or drink. It will taste disgusting and in some cases, such as the Rhubarb leaves it will be toxic.

I recommend you use organic ingredients whenever you can, as many fertilizers and pesticides applied to fruit and vegetables, remain on the skins where they could interact with your dye bath. If you are not able to use organic try scrubbing the outer layers of fruit or vegetables to remove any traces of these products and any dirt.

Enjoy your dyeing experiments!

2 EQUIPMENT LIST

- **Apron or old clothes**
- **Washing up Gloves**
- **Wooden Spoons**
- **Strainers**
- **Muslin cloth bags, old tights or pillow cases – to hold dye materials**
- **Large pans 3 litre capacity.**
- **Glass Jars, containers for excess leftover dye**
- **Funnel**
- **Jam thermometer (optional but good to have if you want to keep very accurate notes)**

Your pans should be large enough to hold your yarn with plenty of space for water around it. If the pan is too cramped the mixture won't have room to move in and around the yarn and you'll end up with a patchy result. Also make sure that the pans you use for dyeing and mordanting are only used for this purpose. Do not mix your dyeing and cooking pans. Where possible it's also a good habit try to dedicate pans to mordanting and another to each colour group to minimize any chance of the colours interacting, for example not dyeing a yellow in your blue pot and accidentally ending up with green because of leftover dye residue.

Collect a selection of muslin cloth bags, old tights and cotton pillow cases to use for submerging your dye materials. This makes them easier to remove from the dye pot than trying to strain a large heavy pot of hot dye mix.

Keep household glass jars, milk cartons or large yoghurt pots aside for storing any dye mix that you do not use on the day. These mixes can be cooled and then stored in the fridge for up to a month.

Set your mordant and dye space up in a well ventilated area or work outside using pots over a fire or portable stove. Make sure you keep pets, children or curious clumsy adults away from your dye pots.

3 MORDANTS

A mordant is an ingredient added your yarn or dye mix that is not the source of the colour. There are many reasons for using a mordant.

- To fix the colour and make the dye stable and longer lasting
- To make a colour brighter
- To make a colour dull
- To interact with the dye mix and change the colour ie in the coffee recipe.

Many natural dye recipes do not require an additional mordant because the dye material naturally contains a form of Tannin. Rhubarb, coffee, tea, onions and avocado's all have a naturally occurring Tannin. Where a mordant has been added to the dye recipe in this book I have used it to boost the fixing of the dye or in some cases to act as a modifier and change the dye colours.

However some people just prefer to mordant yarn and it is a good practice to know about.

Basic Mordant

- Pre-soak your yarn in warm water.
- Mix your mordant ie 12g Alum and 10g Cream of Tartar to 1 litre of water in a large pan.
- Bring the pan to a simmer.
- Squeeze excess water from your yarn, add to the pan and simmer for 1 hour.
- Leave to cool overnight.
- Remove yarn from mix, squeeze excess water.
- Use straight away or dry and store for future use.

I advise adding colour changing mordants ¼ teaspoon at a time to dye mixture so that you can evaluate the effect before adding more. The exact quantity required will vary depending on your own colour preferences and the pH of your dye bath. Some people dye with distilled water or rain water to ensure they are starting from a neutral pH. You can buy pH testing strips to inform yourself of your local water pH point. It is also worth knowing if your water is 'hard' or 'soft', referring to the level of mineral content that is dissolved in it.

The water in Loch Ness is soft but slightly acidic due to the peat on the surrounding hillsides, which also gives the Loch its dark and mysterious colour. The water in my kitchen is soft, with a low mineral content and tends to be very slightly acidic. This generally means my colours are bright and a little mordant goes a long way. If your colours are consistently dull and the coffee dye in this book requires very little mordant to change it is possible that you are in a hard water area. Try dyeing with distilled water to compare the difference.

I encourage you to spend time experimenting with mordants to see the effects for yourself and evaluate the starting point for your water. The general rule is that acids make pinks and alkaline makes blue but it's definitely worth playing for yourself.

You can buy mordant supplies online in powder form or have a go at making your own. Please make sure to store your mordant carefully out of the reach of any pets or children. Making your own takes time and if you intend to follow that process you should start at least one month before you plan to dye.

- **Alum** – this is available in powder form 12g to 1 litre of water (also add 10 g Cream of Tartar). This will make dye mix more acidic and will make some colours appear brighter.

- **Citric acid** – this is available in powder form use 25g to 1 litre of water. You'll probably be used to using a kitchen version of this when you use a squeeze of lemon juice to stop things like apples from turning brown.

- **White vinegar** – available in liquid form from most supermarket, use 1 cup of vinegar to 1 litre of water. This is a weak acid mordant, most often applied during the pre-soaking phase rather than during the dye bath. This opens up the yarn to receive the dye, but be aware it will effect the pH of the dye bath.

- **Ammonia** – this is available in powder form, or you can make your own by collecting your own urine in a glass jar and letting it go stale by exposing to the air for 3-4 weeks. This method using human or animal urine was a traditional mordant for many historical dyers.

- **Iron** – this is available online in powder form, or can be made by collecting old nails in a glass jar covering with water and allowing them to rust over a few weeks. Use 2g of iron to 1 litre of water. This is a strong mordant and should be used sparingly, but has fascinating colour changing powers.

- **Copper** – this is available online in powder form, or can be made by collecting a handful of pennies in a glass jar and covering with water and a splash of vinegar. Use 2 g to 1 litre of water. As with Iron this is a strong mordant and should be used sparingly for beautiful colour changes.

4 PREPARING YOUR YARN

The instructions in this book have been prepared for use with 100% sheep wool yarn. For your own pleasure and interest you may wish to experiment with other fibers such as cashmere or alpaca. These recipes have not been prepared for artificial fibres or plant fibres such as cotton or bamboo, or for silk. Although the process for extracting the dye liquid may be similar plant fibres such as cotton, bamboo, linen, hemp and silk require different preparation and aftercare.

In all dye recipes the yarn should be soaked in lukewarm water for at least 20 minutes before exposing to the dye. This will encourage an even absorption of the dye mixture. If you have previously used an artificial powder known as acid dye mix you may be used to adding some vinegar to this pre-soak mixture. This is to open up the yarn, create a more acidic soaking mixture and promote the take up of those colours. Do not do this with natural dyeing unless specifically instructed, this is because the vinegar will interact with the natural dye to change the pH.

I also encourage you to be wise with your water. The dyeing process uses large quantities of water for pre-soaking, dyeing and rinsing. Every drop of water from your tap has been treated to make it safe for drinking. The water that you use for dyeing does not need this level of treatment. I try to use rain water collected in water butts and water recycled from my condenser tumble dryer to reduce the amount of treated water I'm taking out of and putting back into the water cycle.

When you are ready to dye remove the yarn from the pre-soak and give it a gentle squeeze to remove excess water. You want the yarn to be damp but not soaking wet or dripping. Do not let the yarn dry out completely before adding to the dye mixture or your dye result will be uneven. Avoid transferring the yarn from a cold pre-soak to a hot dye bath as this will shock the yarn and increase the chances of felting. You may be surprised that you can take the temperature of dye baths quite high in order to fix dye. The key is not to move from one extreme to another and NEVER agitate, think very gentle turning not whisking.

After all the dye baths leave the yarn to dry naturally in a shady area, direct sunlight will fade these natural colours more quickly, particularly in the immediate drying time.

5 RED

Reds and pinks are such beautiful yarn colours and one of the loveliest dye baths is made using avocado skins. I'm only using the skins as I encourage you to plant the pits and grow your own for future use. If you would also like to use the pits for dyeing you can mix them with the skins and they will add deeper tones to the dye bath, making pinks more dusky and going through to shades of apricot. For the best chance of reds and pinks choose the darkest purple looking avocados you can find. Skins and pits can be stored in the freezer until you have enough.

The dye instructions given here are for a fresh dye, however I've also had exceptional results from solar dyeing. This involves soaking skins in a large jar or sealed bucket covered in water for 2-4 weeks. I add ammonia or citric acid depending on the colour I am trying to achieve Agitate the mixture daily. If mold appears strain and gently heat before returning to the skins. I find this method works well for my larger scale dyeing as it gives me a reliable low maintenance supply of dye liquid. When I'm ready to dye I simple draw off some liquid, dilute as needed and gently heat to dye.

Party Guacamole
6 avocados
6 spring onions
1 fresh red chilli
2 juicy Limes
Handful of fresh Coriander leaves
Salt

Finely chop the chilli, spring onions and coriander.

Peel and mash your avocados. Putting the skins and pits to one side for dyeing.

Fold in the chilli, onion and coriander mix.

Add the lime juice and salt to taste

Personally I don't like tomato, garlic or sour cream in with my guacamole. I enjoy the creamy taste of pure avocado but if you want to add that other stuff then go for it, it's your guacamole.

This recipe goes beautifully with the Black Bean chilli in Chapter 10.

Avocado Dye
100g yarn
3 litres water
1 cup of white vinegar
25g citric acid – Variable.
200g of avocado skins (more skins to water will make a deeper colour)

Begin by adding vinegar to 1 litre of water for your pre-soak mixture. Add 100g yarn and submerse fully. Soak for at least 20 minutes.

While the yarn is soaking prepare your avocado skins. Make sure all green flesh is removed and cut into strips about 2 cm deep. Cutting the skins allows them to sits more evenly within the water. Add the skins to your large dye pan and cover with 2 litres of water. Add the citric acid and stir until fully dissolved.

Gently heat the avocado and water mix, absolutely no higher than 85 degrees Celsius (185 F). Be gentle with this dye and do not boil, a mild simmering is as exciting as you want to go. Keep the dye mix on this gentle heat for up to 1 hour. Avocado dye is very sensitive to heat and too much takes the dye away from pink and into the brown. So keep a close watch on this pot and if you are happy with the colour before 1 hour please remove from the heat earlier.

Remove pan from the heat and gently strain the liquid to remove the skins, which can be added to your compost heap once cooled. The preserved liquid should be a beautiful colour, ranging from red, dusty pink to apricot. This dye is strong and stable by itself, it does not require the citric acid as a mordant. However by adding it we are encouraging the pink and red tones to come out.

Return the liquid to your pan and continue with the low heat while you finish preparing your yarn. Remove your yarn from the pre-soak. Gently squeeze the excess water and transfer into the large pan.

Continue on the low heat with yarn and dye bath for another 20 minutes. Then remove the pan from the heat and leave the yarn submerged in the dye overnight.

A good avocado bath gives a lot of colour so you may like to reheat and use for another yarn or allow this yarn to dry and then repeat to layer up a richer colour. If the dye bath is not exhausted ie clear you can reserve the remaining dye, allow to cool and store for up to 1 month in the fridge.

If not then simply remove your yarn and rinse in a bowl of cool water to remove the excess dye.
You may like to add another stage with a gentle wool wash to soften and smooth the yarn again before use.

Hang yarn in a shady spot until completely dry.

6 ORANGE

Orange is a beautiful vibrant addition to your yarn basket and easily made from one of the most common kitchen ingredients, onions. Stored onions are better than fresh for crisp dry skins. In this dye I'll use brown onions to gather gorgeous orange tones. Red onions also make beautiful dye, or you an mix the two together. The Onion Marmalade recipe works well with onions of any colour and is gorgeous with strong hard cheese and crackers.

Onion Marmalade
1kg onions
150g caster sugar
3 tbsp red wine vinegar
3 tbsp balsamic vinegar
3 tbsp Port (optional)
2 tbsp olive oil
2 tbsp melted butter

Peel and finely chop the onions. Put the skin to one side for dyeing. They can be stored in a clean dry tub in the cupboard until you have gather enough. Toss a couple of packets of silica gel or a small sachet of rice in the tub to keep the skins dry and prevent them going mouldy during storage.

In a large pan melt the butter and oil together and add the chopped onions.

Heat slowly and gently for 30 minutes until soft and richly brown.

Add the sugar, vinegar and Port. Continue to heat, stirring occasionally for another 30 minutes.

Allow to cool and store in sterile jars.

Onion Dye
200g of onion skins
100g yarn
3 litres water
2 tbsps white vinegar

Begin by pre-soaking 100g of yarn in 1 litre of warm water and a large splash of vinegar, which I estimate to be about 2 tbsps. This dye does not require a mordant as onion skins contain a natural weak tannin. However using an alum or citric acid mordant will give a brighter more vibrant result. See mordant chapter for instructions on preparing a mordant yarn.

Pop your onion skins into a muslin bag and then into a large pan with 2 litres of water. Bring to a simmer and hold there for at least 30 minutes until a rich golden colour has developed.

Remove the skins keeping the dye pan on a low heat.

Remove your yarn from the pre-soak. Gently squeeze the excess water and transfer the yarn into the large pan.

Continue on the low heat with yarn and dye bath for at least 30 minutes. You can keep going up to an hour on the low heat to develop deeper richer colours here.

Remove the pan from the heat and leave the yarn to cool submerged in the dye overnight.

If the dye bath is not exhausted ie clear you can reserve the remaining dye, allow to cool and store for up to 1 month in the fridge.

If not then simply remove your yarn and rinse in a bowl of cool water to remove the excess dye.

You may like to add another stage with a gentle wool wash to soften and smooth the yarn again before use.

Hang yarn in a shady spot until completely dry.

7 YELLOW

A lovely sunny yellow is one of my favorite colors and in the local Highland Gaelic culture this colour is considered lucky. I was delighted when I first saw the sunny golden colours given by Rhubarb leaves in the dye pot. Rhubarb is one of my mums favourite fruits to grow and cook with, so it will always have a place at my table. Rhubarb also grows really well in the Loch Ness area so there are zero air miles in this

Mums Rhubarb Crumble
400 g rhubarb
100g caster Sugar
2 tbsps water or Whisky
100g gluten free plain flour
100g butter (keep it in the fridge)
100g chopped mixed nuts
75 g soft brown sugar

Pre heat oven to 180 Celsius.

Chop rhubarb into small chunks. Putting the leaves to one side for your dye pot.

Toss the rhubarb chunks together with the caster sugar and the whisky or water

Pop into an oven proof dish.

In a separate bowl mix the nuts, soft brown sugar and flour. Then take the butter out the fridge and use a cheese grater to grate it into the mix.

Lightly stir and the butter should pick up the dry ingredients to form tasty little boulders of crunch.

Sprinkle this mixture over the rhubarb to cover.

Pop the lot in the oven for 30 minutes until yummy and golden.

Serve with lashings of custard.

If you're not keen on the whisky flavor try using an orange, ginger syrup or a splash of gin.

Rhubarb Dye
100g yarn
2 litres water
200g of shredded rhubarb leaves.
2 teaspoons baking soda.

Be careful with this dye and work in a well ventilated area. The leaves are toxic and should be disposed of where you are sure that people and pets will not eat them.

Begin by pre-soaking 100g of yarn in 1 litre of warm water. Option to use yarn mordanted with ammonia, see Mordant chapter for basic mordant instructions.

While the yarn is soaking prepare your dye bath. Place 200g of Rhubarb leaves into a muslin bag and pop into your large dye pan and cover with 2 litres of water. Heat to a gentle simmer for up to 30 minutes or until the water is a golden yellow colour.

Carefully remove the bag and preserve the dye liquid. The leaves are now suitable for composting once cool.

Return the dye liquid to your large pan Keeping the pan on a low heat, just less than simmering. Add the baking soda a ¼ teaspoon at a time to intensify the colour of the dye bath. Bear in mind that final yarn will dry to a few shades lighter.

Remove yarn from pre soaking and squeeze out excess water.

Add to the dye bath and submerge for 20 minutes on a low heat.

Remove the pan from the heat and allow to cool overnight with the yarn submerged.

You may need to repeat this process with a second dye bath for a more intense colour.

If the dye bath is not exhausted ie clear you can reserve the remaining dye, allow to cool and store for up to 1 month in the fridge. This mix is high in tannins and if you prepare it without the baking soda will act as a natural mordant for other dyes.

Remove the yarn and rinse the excess dye in a bowl of cool water.

You may wish to add a stage of gentle wool wash to soften the yarn.

Hang in a shady place until completely dry.

8 GREEN

Coffee has become a staple part many morning routines, it's easy to forget how far it travels to reach our shops. So it's great to make the most of all those air miles by using coffee grounds for dyeing.

Coffee is a beautiful strong dye that gives a reliable change of colour. To create green I've used coffee grounds with an iron mordant. Coffee grounds without the iron mordant but with an alum or citric acid mordant will give a beautiful warm golden yellow. The green from this dye has a mossy, sage and sea green quality. Coffee grounds can be stored in the freezer until you have enough for dyeing.

For the recipe I've chosen 4pm muffins with a hit of coffee, cinnamon and dates, the perfect snack for that mid-afternoon slump.

4pm muffins
300g gluten free self raising flour
150g yoghurt
1 cup cold black coffee
150g dry dates
40g golden caster sugar
1 teaspoon cinnamon or unsweeted cocoa powder
2 eggs
Pinch salt

Pre heat oven to 180 Celsius. Line your muffin tray with muffin cases.

Chop the dates in half and soak in the coffee.

Mix the dry ingredients together. Whisk the wet ingredients together in separate bowl.

Gently add the wet to the dry. Drain and fold in the soaked dates.

Pour into muffin cases until they are ½ full.

Pop into the oven for 15 to 20 minutes, until a skewer comes out clean. Be careful because this dark mixture will fool you into thinking it is ready before it really is.

Remove from oven and leave to cool before serving.

Coffee Dye
100g yarn
3 litres water
¼ teaspoon Iron mordant
200g of coffee grounds.

Begin by pre-soaking 100g of yarn in 1 litre of warm water.

While the yarn is soaking prepare your coffee ground dye bath. Place 200g of coffee grounds into a muslin bag and submerge in 2 litres of water in your large pan. Heat to a simmer for up to 30 minutes.

Remove the coffee grounds, these are now suitable for composting once cool. Your pan should now contain a large quantity of the coffee coloured dye.

Keeping the pan on a low heat, just less than simmering. Begin to add the iron mordant a few grains at a time, and give it a really good stir. Iron is a strong mordant and you may not need the full amount to reach an agreeable shade of green.

Remove yarn from pre soaking and squeeze out excess water.

Add to the dye bath and submerge for 20 minutes on a low heat.

Coffee is a strong dye bath, for a paler colour remove the yarn after 20 minutes. For a deeper colour remove the pan from the heat and allow to cool overnight with the yarn. If the dye bath is not exhausted ie clear you can reserve the remaining dye, allow to cool and store for up to 1 month in the fridge.

Remove the yarn and rinse the excess dye in a bowl of cool water.

Some types of coffee seem to leave a residue on the yarn and may require more than one rinse.

You may wish to add a stage of gentle wool wash to soften the yarn.

Hang in a shady place until completely dry.

9 BLUE

Moving into the blue range of the colour spectrum it is helpful to learn about Anthocyanins. These are naturally occurring compounds that give plants deep purple and red colours, and antioxidant properties. There are a wide choice of purple plants that are easy to grow or find in your local supermarket; red cabbage, cherries, raspberries, redcurrant, blueberry and blackcurrants.

Red cabbage is pH sensitive, experiment by adding small amounts of ammonia or baking soda to get a really gorgeous teal green colour as an alternative to the dull green in the previous chapter. If you'd like to intensify the pink and purple elements of the red cabbage try adding Citric Acid.

This dye is a great way to use those outer leaves of a cabbage that are sometimes a bit ragged. They can be shredded and stored in the freezer until 200g has been collected. However for dyeing I would recommend drying the red cabbage in a sunny sport, a dehydrator or overnight in a fan oven at 55 degrees Celsius (135F) to pull the moisture out of the cabbage and maximize the anthocyanin content. Then store the dried cabbage in a dark jar until you have collected sufficient quantities.

Christmas Cabbage
1 red cabbage
2tbsp olive oil
2tbsp butter
2tbsp red wine vinegar
2 tbsp Port or balsamic vinegar
1 jar cranberry sauce (or 100g fresh cranberries and 2 tbsp of soft brown sugar)

Remove the outer leaves and core of the cabbage place to one side for drying or freezing.

Shred the remaining cabbage.

Gently heat oil and butter in a large saucepan Add the shredded cabbage stir for a couple of minutes until coated in the melted oil and butter.

Add the vinegar and Port. Heat low and slow for about 40 minutes

Stir in the cranberry sauce and gently heat for another couple of minutes until everything is combined and looking shiny and sticky.
Serves up great with roast dinners, sausages and rich nutty savory bakes.

Red cabbage dye
100g yarn
2 litres water
200g of shredded dried red cabbage.
2 teaspoons baking soda.

Begin by pre-soaking 100g of yarn in 1 litre of warm water.

While the yarn is soaking prepare your red cabbage dye bath. Place 200g of dried red cabbage into a muslin bag and pop into your large dye pan and cover with 2 litres of water. Heat to a gentle simmer for up to 30 minutes or until the water is a deep purple colour, much darker than you think it needs to be.

Carefully strain the red cabbage and preserve the dye liquid. The red cabbage is now suitable for composting once cool.

Return the dye liquid to your large pan Keeping the pan on a low heat, just less than simmering. Add the baking soda a ¼ teaspoon at a time to change the colour of the dye bath. The more you add the greener the liquid will be, although bear in mind that final yarn will dry to a few shades lighter.

Remove yarn from pre soaking and squeeze out excess water.

Add to the dye bath and submerge for 20 minutes on a low heat.

Remove the pan from the heat and allow to cool overnight with the yarn submerged.

This dye appears dark when wet but as it dries will fade to a baby blue colour. This is called a Cyanotic change, similar to forming a bruise. You may need to repeat this process with a second dye bath for a more intense colour.

If the dye bath is not exhausted ie clear you can reserve the remaining dye, allow to cool and store for up to 1 month in the fridge.

Remove the yarn and rinse the excess dye in a bowl of cool water.
You may wish to add a stage of gentle wool wash to soften the yarn.

Hang in a shady place until completely dry.

10 INDIGO AND VIOLET

Indigo and violet are combined here as the two often overlap in dye result. The avocado dye at the start of this book created warm pink with red, brown and orange undertones. At this end of the colour spectrum we are aiming for the violet range of pink, purple and lavender which have cool blue undertones.

True indigo and violet are most reliable from artificial sources, in the natural world the most well known dye sources are the Woad *Isatis tinctoria* or Indigo *Indigofera* plant species. Unfortunately for my dyeing neither of these sources are edible or commonly found around Loch Ness. Alternative sources of Indigo are hard to find in the kitchen, as intense bright blue is one of nature's Aposematic or warning colours indicating toxicity.

I've found that black rice and black turtle beans both contain high levels of anthocyanins and give great results from the soaking water, meaning I can still use the rice and beans for cooking afterwards. Black rice is an heirloom variety of rice that has a lovely sweet nutty flavor and makes a stunning addition to your kitchen table. The rice is naturally high in iron and fibre. Black turtle beans have filling hearty flavor that is great for big pots of comfort chilli and burritos.

Black Rice Rice pudding
150g black rice
150g full fat coconut milk
4 cups water
75g sugar

Place the rice in a large pan and cover with 2 cups of water. Leave to soak for a minimum of 30 minutes. Ideally you soak the rice grains overnight and then make this as a breakfast dish.

Strain the rice and reserve the coloured liquid for dyeing. You can store the coloured rice water in the fridge until you have enough for dyeing.

Return the rice to the pan and cover with the remaining water.

Stir in the sugar and coconut milk.

Heat on low until all the water has been absorbed 20-40minutes. The rice should be cooked but still have texture and shape.

Serve as a warm breakfast alternative to porridge, as a dessert or cold if you like that kind of thing.

Suggested toppings – toasted nut, berries, fresh mango, banana chips, coconut shavings.

Black Rice Dye
100g yarn
1 litres water for pre-soaking
2 litres of water kept from the rice soaking.
6g or 2 teaspoons baking soda (optional)

Begin by pre-soaking 100g of yarn in 1 litre of warm water.

While the yarn is soaking prepare your rice water dye bath. Pour the 2 litres of rice water into your large pan. Keeping the pan on a low heat, just less than simmering. This dye gives a strong colour change ranging from deep red/purple to lavender greys. I enjoy using it with or without the colour change.
Begin to add the baking soda ¼ teaspoon at a time. Baking soda reacts strongly with this dye bath and you may not need the full amount to reach an agreeable purple/lavender shade.

Remove yarn from pre soaking and squeeze out excess water.

Add to the dye bath and submerge for 20 minutes on a low heat.

Remove the pan from the heat and allow to cool overnight with the yarn submerged.

Remove the yarn and rinse the excess dye in a bowl of cool water. Allow to dry in the shade and repeat until the dye bath is exhausted or you are happy with the shade. You may even wish to repeat with a second dye bath.

If the dye bath is not exhausted ie clear you can reserve the remaining dye, allow to cool and store for up to 1 month in the fridge.

You may wish to add a stage of gentle wool wash to soften the yarn.

Hang in a shady place until completely dry.

Black Bean Chilli
2 onions
225 g dried black turtle beans
2 tins tomatoes
2 tbsp cider, balsamic or red wine vinegar
2tbsp oil
2 garlic cloves
2 tbsp spice mix

Dried spice mix (can be made in advance and stored in your spice cupboard)
2tbsp chilli powder
2 tsp cacao powder
2 tsp paprika
2tsp smoked paprika
1tsp cumin
1tsp coriander
½ tsp garlic powder
½ tsp cayenne
½ tsp salt

Soak the black beans overnight. Reserve the water for your dye pot using a ladle rather than a colander to strain. Cover with fresh water and boil up for 10minutes. Then drain for use in the chilli.

Peel and finely slice the garlic and onions. Saving your onion skins for future dyeing.

Add the oil to a large pan and gently soften the onions and garlic. Add the vinegar and cook on low until the onions are very soft.

Add spice mix and gently combine to form a paste.

Add one tin of tomatoes, then the beans, then the 2nd tin of tomatoes. You really want everything to combine evenly in the pot but be gentle or the beans will breakdown and this will end up as really tasty mush.

Keep cooking for an hour. If the mix still looks a bit dry you can add additional water, or beer or wine to suit your taste. We used to make this with Loch Ness Brewery Smokie Ness Rocking Red Ale, but that's been discontinued.

This last part can be done on the hob, in a covered dish in the oven or in a slow cooker.

Serve with rice and guacamole from Chapter 1. This chilli often tastes even better on day 2 as leftovers.

Black Bean Dye
100g yarn
1 litres water
25g citric acid.
1 litre black bean liquid

Begin by adding an acidic mordant to your pre-soak mixture. Mix citric acid 1 litre of warm water. Stir until fully dissolved. Add 100g yarn and immerse fully. Soak for at least 20 minutes.

While the yarn is soaking prepare your dye. Strain the reserved black bean soaking water into your large pan to remove all beans or fibers. Pay attention to ensure these are totally removed as they effect the end dye colour.

Simply place the yarn into the pan and leave for at least 24 hours. The initial colour of the dye and yarn does not reflect the final colour, so be patient leave it alone for as long as you can bear.

This dye does not need heat, just a spot on the window ledge to do its thing. I use this low maintenance and low energy solar dye method with most of my dyes as it is so easy to set up and leave.

Remove your yarn and rinse in a bowl of cool water to remove the excess dye. This dye is very sensitive to pH, try testing it with your tap water and collected rain water to see if you can tell the difference.

Repeat as needed to achieve your preferred depth of colour.

If the dye bath is not exhausted ie clear you can reserve the remaining dye, allow to cool and store for up to 1 month in the fridge.

You may like to add another stage with a gentle wool wash to soften and smooth the yarn again before use.

Hang yarn in a shady spot until completely dry.

ABOUT THE AUTHOR

Dwynwen is the owner and creator of Loch Ness Knitting based in Drumnadrochit near Loch Ness. Dwynwen runs regular workshops on natural dyeing and produces hand dyed yarns, knitting patterns, and knitted items to sell to visitors in the Loch Ness area from her studio in the Drumnadrochit village. Dwynwen and her husband Toby work together to produce Loch Ness Living, a YouTube channel telling the story behind some of the other small businesses, creative people and inspirational places in the Loch Ness area.

Manufactured by Amazon.ca
Bolton, ON